Manifestes
3

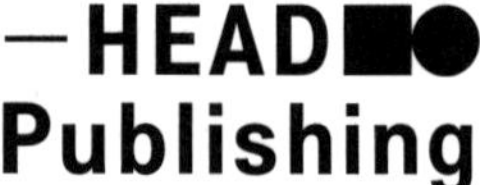

Jill Gasparina
Christophe Kihm
Anne-Lyse Renon

Ways to Leave Earth

The nine texts that make up this collective work all attempt to answer a single question—how to leave Earth—via a material and sensory approach to habitability. Each considers problems related to extra-terrestrial living from the starting point of objects of increasing size, starting with the astronaut's glove and ranging up to the exoplanet. Their perspective is critical of the kind of functional conception of habitability broadly accepted in space studies: one that is based on technological rationality and its ability to resolve questions of adaptation to a hostile environment, and addresses requirements in terms of productivity and quality of life for its inhabitants.

We, on the other hand, take the view that there is more than one way of living in space, and that each habitability is a complex reflection of our attachments and dependencies. To experience space is to undergo a radical change of surroundings: one that alters perceptions and actions and allows us to break free from anthropocentric models of adaptation.

How can we embrace those externalities, what sensory relationships to those worlds outside can we construct, and how can we adapt our senses to cope with alienation? How do these attachments to something completely different lead us to develop alternative skills and forms of knowledge, both physical and social?

This perspective on forms of habitability in space may be described as extra-Earthly because, in contrast to the functional logic of adaptation of and to an environment, it does not involve projecting the terrestrial into space. In re-situating the Earth as a unique place within the cosmos, it turns the universalist point of view on its head and encourages us to rediscover our ties to all existing things on Earth, from outside. The ways in which we might live far away from Earth are therefore an opportunity to rethink the ways we live on Earth, starting from that 'estrangement' or alienation from ourselves, and the defamiliarisation of everything around us.

The need for humans to protect themselves against the space environment first came to the fore during the Russian and American missions of the 1950s and 1960s, with the Soyuz and Gemini programmes. Since then, the issues involved in human space flight have been further clarified in the course of the Vostok, Apollo and Skylab programmes, and on to the age of the Space Shuttle and the Salyut, Mir and ISS space stations. Over the decades, the spacesuit glove has evolved into a complex component of the extravehicular mobility unit (EMU). It has undergone vast improvements in mobility and dexterity, which are vital to the conditions for life and activity, especially in space.

The David Clark Company, which had designed suits for US aviation since the early 1940s, developed the first prototype pressure suits for the US Air Force in the 1950s and 1960s. It supplied the first, the MC-2, for the Mercury project: the gloves were permanently attached to the upper rubberised garment, but were heavily criticised

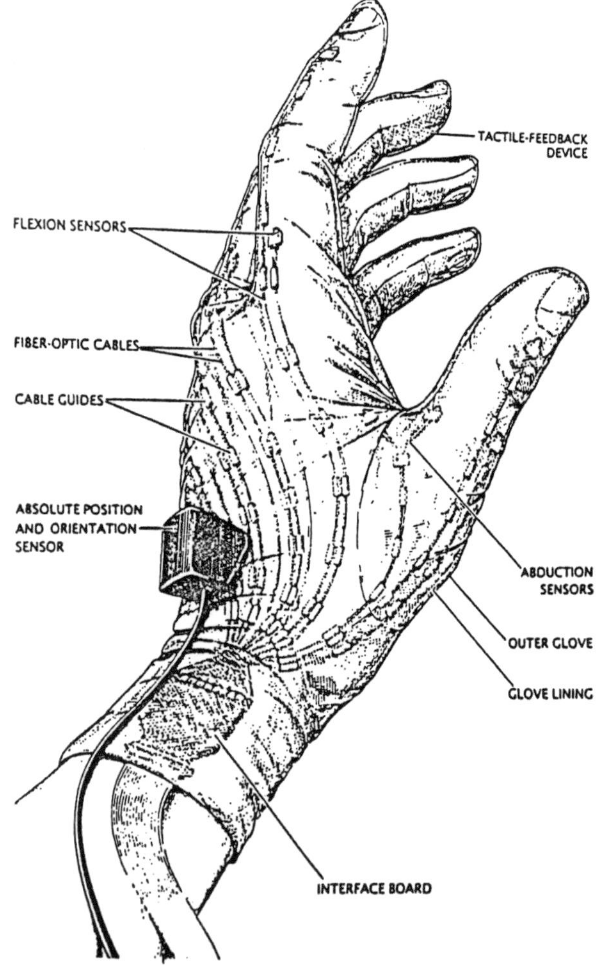

DATAGLOVE developed by VPL Research, Inc., translates hand and finger movements into electrical signals. Between two layers of cloth, fiber-optic cables anchored at both ends to an interface board run the length of each finger and double back. Each cable has a light-emitting diode at one end and a phototransistor at the other. Cables are treated so that light escapes when a finger flexes; the phototransistor converts the light it receives into an electrical signal. The position and orientation sensor is made by the Polhemus Navigation Sciences division of the McDonnell Douglas Corporation.

by pilots. Despite changes to the quality of the leather, the problems of moisture and pressure build-up remained. When NASA engineers refined the suit on the way to creating the improved A/P22S-2, they therefore resolved to design removable gloves that would offer general comfort and ease of donning. Removing the gloves also prevented excessive moisture from accumulating and made it easier for pilots to take off their suits themselves if need be. Another advantage was that a punctured glove could be changed without having to replace the entire suit.

From these beginnings, many of the tasks carried out by astronauts have come to be structured around the existing capacities of the gloves, and six basic characteristics have been identified: degree of movement, strength, tactility, dexterity, fatigue and comfort (Abts, 1999).

Phalanges, fingers, palms, pincers and fists impose limits on the articulation of gestures, which are completely reconceived to accommodate the technical constraints of the gloves worn by astronauts, in accordance with two main criteria:

- Because the glove does not allow for the same delicacy of movement as the hand's articulation apparatus, astronauts must select the best way to grasp an object and establish a hierarchy of movements. Every time astronauts handle an object as part of a technical task, they must choose the space in which they will do so.

- Unlike mass, volume and surface, technology is not intrinsic to an object. Movements and uses constrained by the space environment tie objects to new technologies but also to new knowledge that necessitates new forms of gesture.

Human beings' strength, dexterity, ability to manipulate and tactile perception are unique. They make hands an efficient, multi-purpose tool, rendering the human body superior to artificial devices when it comes to adaptive and complex tasks that cannot be wholly defined in advance. Consequently, gloves for extravehicular activities (EVA) are the main (and sometimes only) interface between the astronaut and the work they have to do; they must therefore strike a balance between mobility, tactile comfort and protection against the dangers of the space environment.

The difficulty of grasping objects while wearing gloves is a recurring problem for astronauts engaging in extravehicular activities. The glove is made of several layers of plastic to prevent air from escaping. The fabric gives it strength to ensure that the plastic does not split and also offers insulation and protection against micrometeors. All these factors restrict the design of flexible gloves, which may have good sensory capacities, but grasping objects through all the layers or with rubber and plastic fingertips remains a complex operation. Another, even more significant problem is astronauts becoming tired through the effort needed to move the glove from its neutral position[1] because of the differences in pressure between the inside of the spacesuit and the space environment on the outside. Every movement, such as gripping, squeezing or extending the fingers, entails physical exertion. To establish a scale of sensations for space applications, miniature force sensors on the glove palm were envisaged as early as 1987 that would drive an electrotactile belt around the waist, thus augmenting the missing tactile sensation (Bach-Y-Rita *et al.*, 1987).

Sensory substitution systems have been, or are being, developed. Tactile vision is a phenomenon observed, for example, in the mobilisation of attention between the blind man and his stick, which may be regarded as his 'seeing finger' (Malafouris, 2013), while in the same way auditory and somato-sensory substitution for hands and feet that have lost their sense of touch is currently being studied. The RoboGlove project, developed by the Swedish company Bioservo in 2016, combines a glove containing sensors with a robotic exoskeleton that amplifies and adds precision to the movements of the hands inside the glove. This project is one of the innovations designed with a view to missions to Mars, with robot assistance mitigating the deficit of tactile sensation. Synaesthetic prototypes (Talvi, 2019) which aim to combine the interaction between a number of senses

1   When the glove is positioned on the suit, it is said to be in its 'neutral' position, i.e. a position typically adopted by the hand when not subject to external influences.

in addition to touch, along with automated exo-skeletons, share this goal of enabling astronauts to interact better with their environment. They are a response to the requirements of 'tactile value', which involves economy of movement and of means. However, the development of certain physical aptitudes via the sensitivity of the epidermis cannot be achieved solely through sensory substitution. If we are to live in space, we will need to 'educate our sense of touch', as Marinetti proposed in his manifesto of 'tactilism' (Marinetti, 1921).

THE DIVING SUIT
AS MOBILE HABITAT

The very first pressurised, high-altitude suit, designed by Wiley Post and Russell Colley of the B. F. Goodrich Company, was used for flights into the stratosphere in 1934 and 1935. These earliest suits were partially or entirely rigid, offering substantial protection against radiation while ensuring that vital needs were met and allowing the wearer to interact with the environment. However, they vastly restricted freedom of manoeuvre, owing to the lack of space in the pilots' cockpits and habitable modules on board, and the technical specifications (De Monchaux, 2011).

The suit currently in use in the US, the EMU (Extravehicular Mobility Unit), is essentially an anthropomorphic enclosure, a technological envelope weighing 127 kg and comprising an adaptable, modular suit and tailor-made gloves that humans can use to work in the space environment (Young and Avino, 2009). It consists of a complex, multi-layered, high-technology, pressurised system. Ever since human beings first walked on

[Fig. 2] Degrees of freedom in the tree model of the DataSuit, VPL Research Inc.

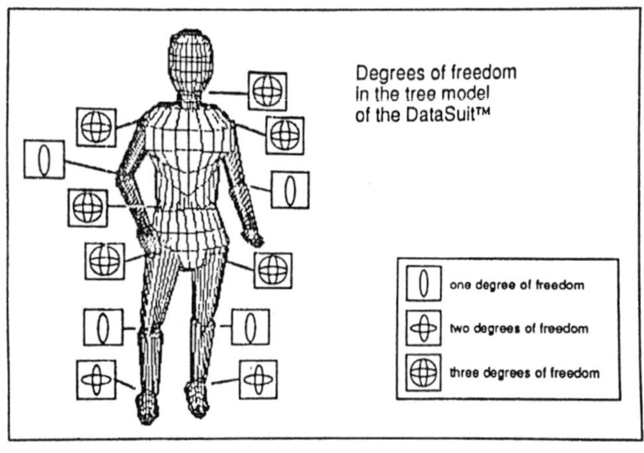

[Fig. 3] EVA System and EVA Reference Configuration, presentation of the Hermes Quick System, April 1992, p.83

5.3. EVA System

5.3.1. EVA Reference Configuration

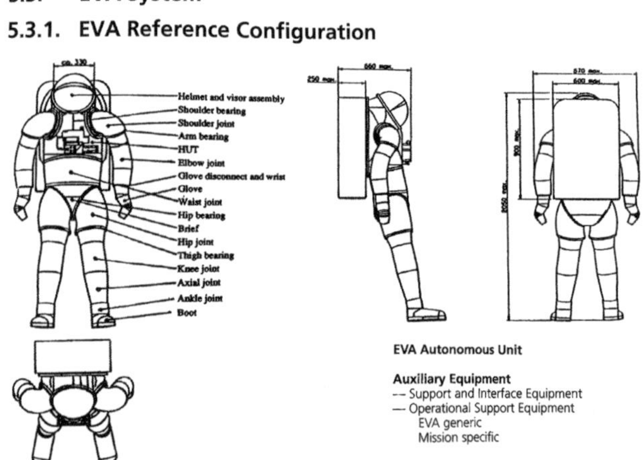

the Moon in 1969, this form of habitat-cum-outfit has caused problems of autonomy and weight. It is designed to assist a human body, but it also has the effect of seriously restricting its mobility in space and limiting its dexterity. In fact, it requires adaptation to microgravity and weightlessness, and depends on a reconfiguration of the intuitions and reflexes of sensory life on Earth (Shepard *et al.*, 1973).

As far back as 1966, Buzz Aldrin suggested using deep-sea diving to train astronauts for life in space (Marlier and Mouriaux, 2017). Although it can in no way replicate the precise conditions of weightlessness, the resistance of the water means that the neutral buoyancy of such dives allows us to conceive the anthropometry of these habitat/outfits in terms of a relationship between relearning physical techniques such as walking, jumping and moving around on the one hand, and constantly changing cognitive operations on the other. Aside from parabolic flights, which are of very short duration, training in a swimming pool is therefore an essential way of familiarising oneself with these new physical living conditions.

A European programme to train the astronauts of the future was launched in 1980, linked to the development—subsequently abandoned—of the Hermes shuttle, and tested since then by many astronauts from ESA to Comex[2] in Marseille (Marlier and Mouriaux, 2017). Innovations and evolutions in the habitability of space suits have been implemented, notably with the development of amphibious training suits designed with a view to future voyages to the Moon and Mars. The idea is to investigate astronauts' motor ability in this aquatic analogue, using technological tools that both assist and restrict mobility, and to study how the senses adapt to extravehicular missions.

An early training suit named Gandolfi is initially developed by Comex in 1988, with the aim of replicating the characteristics of mobility in space in terms of bulk, microgravity and field of view. It is followed in 2016 by the Gandolfi 2 model. Part of the Moonwalk project headed by Peter Weiss, Director of the Space and Innovation Department at Comex, it employs the principle of the exoskeleton with adjustable constraints on the limbs. Ventral and lateral belts allow it to adjust to the astronaut's size. The resistance caused by inflation (to simulate a vacuum or low pressure) can be regulated, and ball bearings or similar devices enable the arms, legs and pelvis to rotate.

Placed in the living and working conditions of the analogue, the astronaut begins by carrying out simulations of extravehicular activities from

2   Comex (Compagnie Maritime d'Expertise) is an engineering company specialising in human interventions in extreme environments. It develops models for underwater exploration and robotics.

3   The principle of enaction ('causing to emerge through action') was proposed by Francisco Varela in the 1980s. It denotes 'a property that certain systems have of constructing themselves, permanently and through interaction with their environment.' (Benoît Le Blanc, 'Francisco Varela: des systèmes et des boucles', in *Hermès, La Revue,* vol. 68, no. 1, 2014, p. 106–107)

the SHEE (Self-deployable Habitat for Extreme Environments). This unit is itself intended to replicate the living, working and socialising conditions of space, while interacting with the constraints of the suit's envelope in a confined area, either on the Moon or Mars, and with the external robotic material.

The goal is not simply to adapt the body to the habitat but also to create technological devices that enable experiences of space and immersiveness in a variety of modes (tactile, auditory, emotional, and so on). Within the environment, or through the characteristics of the technical apparatus, it should be possible to provide sensory feedback of the kind studied in a range of scenarios involving interaction with virtual, augmented or mixed reality applications (Zhang, Zadtootaghaj, Hoel, Perkis, 2018).

Another perspective on the sensorimotor adaptability of astronauts, with an eye to upcoming crewed space flights and, in particular, the ambition to establish colonies in space, comes from studies into ways of integrating the human system into complex human-machine and robotic devices. Reproducing gestures in a state of weightlessness, learning to interact with the environment and living in space involve more than adaptation. In other words, astronauts will have to get to grips with suits that are no longer just envelopes but rather embedded technological and cognitive systems based on the principle of enaction[3], in line with sensorimotor approaches to cognition which postulate that both the body and its environment adapt to each other (Colombetti, 2010).

As Manfred E. Clynes and Nathan S. Kline noted as far back as 1960: 'Altering man's bodily functions to meet the requirements of extra-terrestrial environments would be more logical than providing an earthly environment for him in space... Artifact-organism systems which would extend man's unconscious, self-regulatory controls are one possibility.'[4]

4   Manfred E. Clynes, a researcher specialising in dynamic simulation, and Nathan S. Kline, a director of research specialising in psychiatry, published an article in 1960 entitled 'Cyborgs and Space', which remains famous to this day. In it, they popularised the term 'cyborg', to denote a human body technologically enhanced to enable it to survive in space.

In the popular science fiction of the 1950s, the rockets that convey human beings on their conquest of space can usually be recognised by their monobloc, streamlined appearance, like an elongated cigar with a pointed nose. This generic form of rocket, found everywhere from *Destination Moon* (1950) and the illustrations of Hergé to the covers of pulp fiction, is derived from the shape of the V–2. A ballistic missile developed from 1936 onwards by engineers working for Nazi Germany under the leadership of Wernher von Braun, the V–2 makes its first successful flight in 1942. Mass-produced by prisoners in the Dora concentration camp, it is launched against Paris, London and Antwerp in 1944.

The V–2 enjoys mythical status in the history of both weapons and the Second World War, as the weapon that ought to have won the conflict for the Nazis. Initially referred to as the A4 (Aggregat 4), it is renamed V–2, *Vergeltungswaffe* 2, or 'Vengeance Weapon 2' by Himmler in 1942

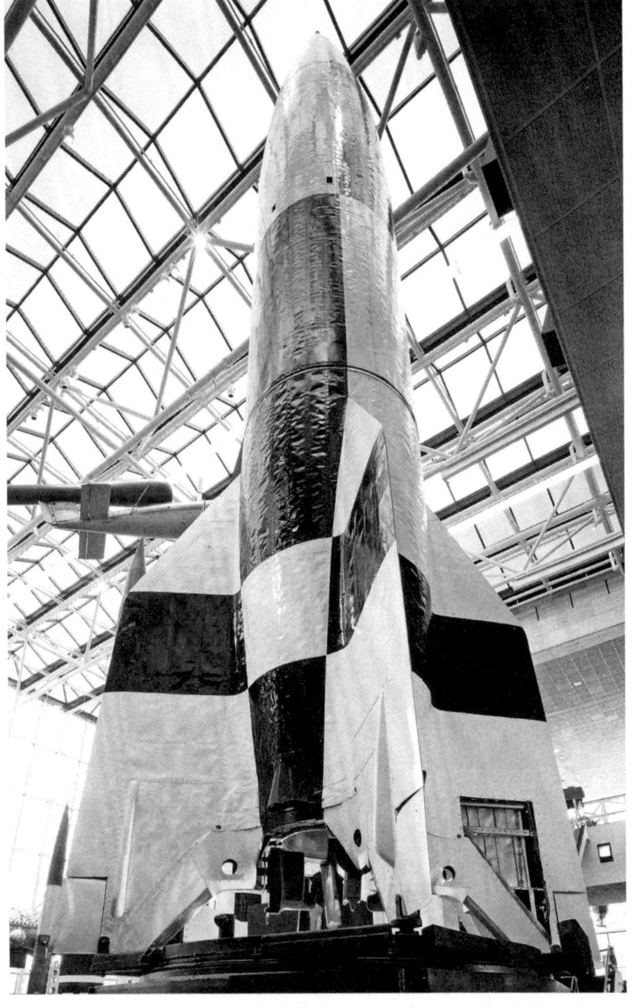

[Fig. 4] **V–2 missile, 'Space Race' gallery,
National Air and Space Museum,
Washington**

(Neufeld, 2008; Newell, 2019). In essence, it is designed to inflict psychological terror as much as physical destruction. Not only is it the biggest, heaviest and most powerful rocket in the world at the time (Winter, 1983), but its supersonic speed renders it silent, allowing it to strike without warning.

However, guiding it proves difficult and its deployment in the field ends in debacle. In no time at all, the V–2 goes extra-terrestrial: it becomes the first human-made object to reach space when, in June 1944, it achieves an altitude of more than 100 km. In this respect, it is considered the forerunner of all launchers, and especially Redstone and Saturn V (Le Maner, 2007). When the war ends, the missile's function is radically transformed. In 1946, the US Army uses a V–2 to send spores and mushrooms into space as part of biological experiments into the impact of radiation. In 1949, a monkey named Albert is on board as both passenger and experimental subject. Back in 1947, the Americans used a V–2 to photograph the Earth from space for the first time in history, while in the mid–1940s, Arthur C. Clarke even imagines it being used to put a communications satellite into orbit. Within five years, the V–2 morphs from weapon of mass destruction into space vehicle, and from allegory of terror into a welcome, peaceful—and widely replicated—symbol of the promise of space.

While a study of its history sheds light on the mechanisms of this progressive demilitarisation,

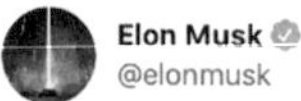

Starship test flight rocket just finished assembly at the @SpaceX Texas launch site. This is an actual picture, not a rendering.

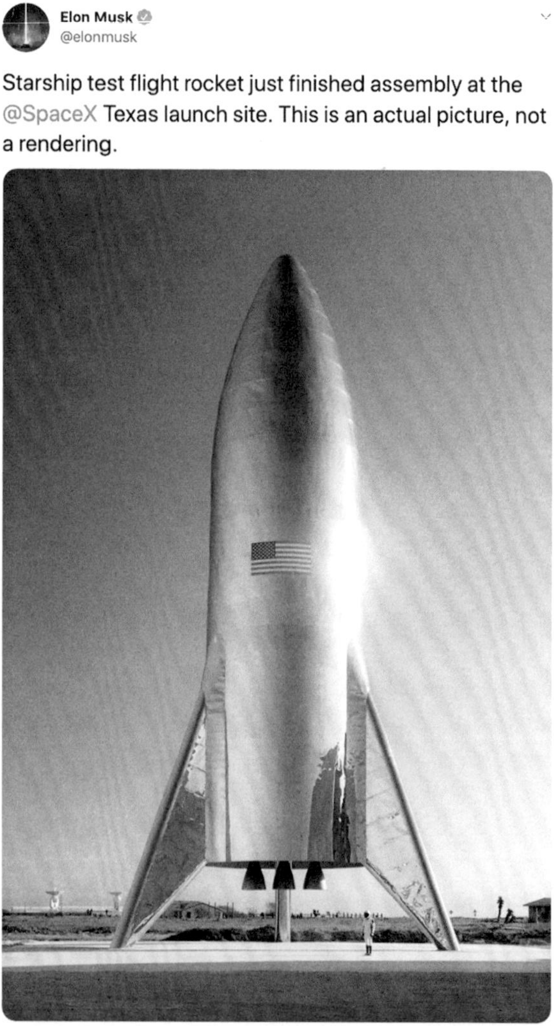

the changes in the V–2's function open up a number of avenues of research with regard to the design of space habitats. Over time, the V–2 acquires a whole range of functions: not just missile and launcher but also habitat (not to mention cultural icon). Projects to convert the missile into an inhabited rocket are envisaged from the earliest stages of its development (Winter, 1983). In the late 1940s, the engineer Harry Ross of the British Interplanetary Society proposes the idea of the Megaroc, a V–2 adapted to carry humans (Macauley, 2012). Von Braun later works on the ferry rocket. But while we wait for news of success from the SpaceX Starship—an idea seemingly straight out of von Braun's imaginings—the only place where V–2s are launched into space is in the pages of fiction: capsules attached to the nose of the launchers have proven the only way to accommodate humans, rather than putting them in the body of the rocket itself. In fact, however, this strategy of repurposing a pre-existing structure to act as a habitat is a recurring feature in the history of space exploration. The main module of Skylab, for instance, is based on the third stage of the giant Saturn V lunar rocket. Over at the ISS, the FGB Zarya module is derived from the TKS spacecraft, the first element of the ISS to be launched, in 1998. Space architecture is therefore also an architecture of transformation (Rambert, 2015).

The proliferation of functions can also occur synchronously: when von Braun first announced his project for a station orbiting in space, he envisages it not primarily as a habitat, but rather as having a host of military, scientific, strategic and diplomatic functions ranging from 'instrument of peace' to 'weapon' of mass destruction and 'trampoline for space exploration' (von Braun, 1952, p. 22-39, 65-74). The Space Shuttle, meanwhile, was conceived as a living environment, laboratory and vehicle, and this was reflected in the organisation of its interior spaces. As for the ISS, it is now not just a habitat but also a laboratory, an observatory—and a great place to take selfies. This multifunctionality reflects the marginal significance accorded to space architectures' function as habitats—admirably summed up in the expression 'man in a can' used by the first astronauts. It also reveals a historical phenomenon, a very progressive quest to make these architectures habitable (Häuplik-Meusburger, 2011; Song Lockard, 2015). Thanks to its 'dual' (Le Maner, 2007, p. 121) character, the V-2 was destined to undergo multiple changes of function.

The V-2's fate in popular fiction, meanwhile, brings us to another, very different problem. With its 'image of aerodynamic grace' (McCurdy, 2011, p. 217) and perfectly modern silhouette, the V-2 embodied the fantasy of human space flight at least until the Shuttle came along. And as with the orbiting space station—a visual icon of the 1950s to 1970s—the massive phenomena of appropriation, derivation and transformation that this vehicle experienced on its way to becoming pure image or pure bloc can serve as a starting point for a reflection on the medium of images. Who are the agents disseminating the form? Are there 'image boosters', whose role in spreading an image is similar to that of the 'space boosters' described by Howard McCurdy? What are we to make of the fact that this iconic form's Nazi origins have been airbrushed from the universalist productions of pop culture? 'The architecture of the future will be a missile' (Fontana, [1952] 2013), Lucio Fontana prophesied in his 1952 work 'Why I Am a Spatialist', written at a time when science fiction's infatuation with the V-2 was at its height. As we attempt to reconcile this weapon of war's dual evolutions into both pop icon and habitat, we may note that what makes them possible is a common act of visual appropriation and cultural domestication: the addition of a door or a porthole to an image. Thus the modernist sculptural model of the autonomous form enclosed upon itself is converted into a dynamic architecture, and a space rendered habitable by and through images.

[Fig. 6] **Project Mercury Familiarisation Manual. Manned Satellite Capsule, Cabin Equipment (Figure 1–5. Sheet 1 of 2), p. 17. McDonnell Aircraft Corporation / NASA, 15 December 1959**

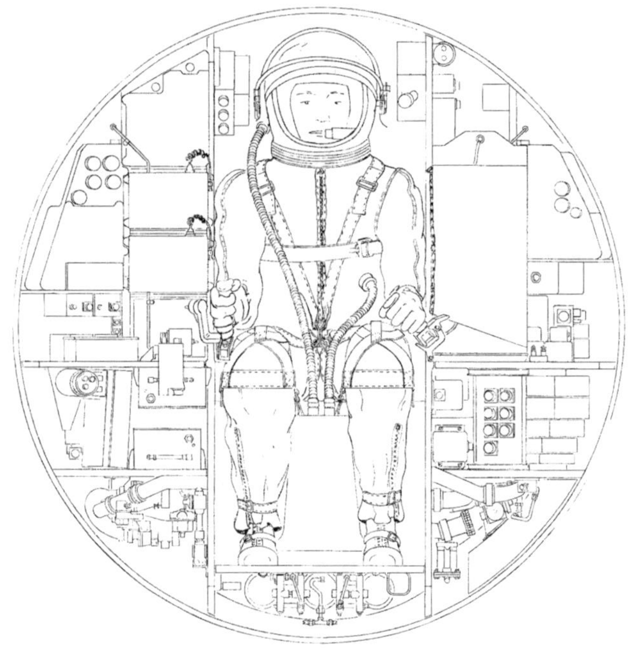

It is easy to forget, given its centrality to our experiences, that gravity dictates the potential of our actions, motions, postures and the positions of our bodies on the Earth's surface. Once those coordinates are redefined, as they are under the conditions of speed and distance produced by flight and life in space, numerous material arrangements need to be made to accommodate bodies and their actions and respond to the changes of surroundings.

The designer Raymond Loewy is credited with inventing floor restraint systems that were used on the Skylab space station (launched in 1973) to keep the astronauts' bodies in place while orbiting in zero gravity. The floor and ceiling of Skylab were covered with grids machined from sheets of aluminium that provided handholds and footholds for the astronauts as they floated around the craft's interior. The astronauts' shoes, meanwhile, were fitted with cleats which they could slot into the cutouts and so fix their bodies to a surface (Sgobba and Schlacht, 2018).

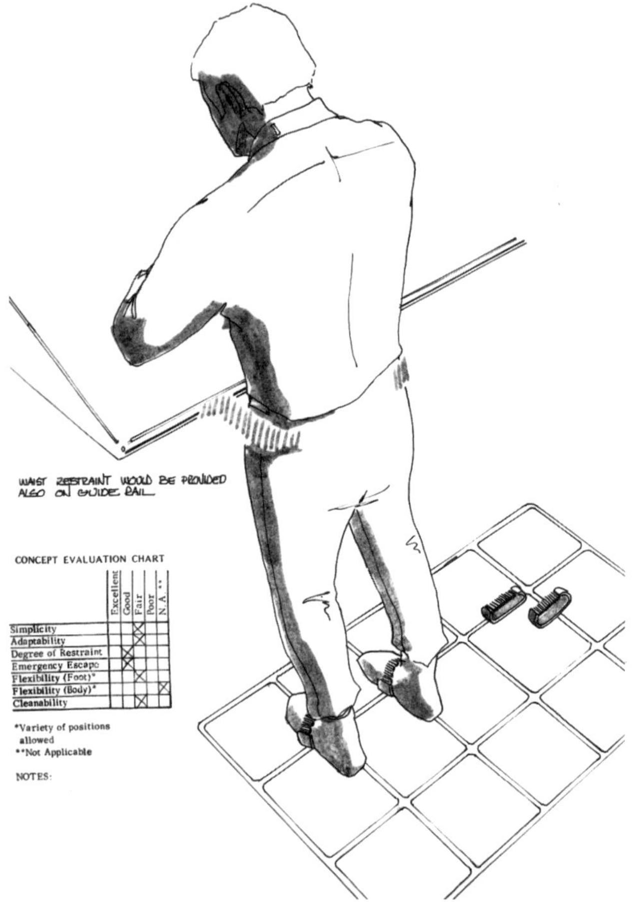

[Fig. 7] **Raymond Loewy, restraint system for Skylab (commissioned by NASA), 1972**

Inside space habitats—both vehicular and stationary—restraint systems such as fabric straps, loops, footrests, grips and handrails are essential to articulating the displacements of bodies in space and enabling various activities to be carried out. The variety of such mechanisms reflects positions and practices associated with tasks and how long they take, from the simplest actions such as eating a meal to more complex operations. The number of holds is proportional to the volume of the habitat and the dimensions of its surfaces, which in turn are dictated by the length of time the craft spends in space; and that number defines an ergonomics. The rhythm imposed by these attachments on the surfaces of those habitats, and their locations, can be categorised as elements of habitability inasmuch as they signify the environment by the action possibilities they offer—their 'affordances'.[5]

These material requirements to attach bodies under extra-terrestrial physical conditions can apply to both vehicles and space habitats. On the 30th May 2020, the private company SpaceX launched its first crewed space flight, with two NASA astronauts on board the capsule of the Dragon spacecraft, located at the tip of the Falcon 9 rocket. Although private operators have only recently become involved in commercial crewed space flight,

5   First elaborated by James J. Gibson in 1966, the concept of affordance denotes what an environment provides or furnishes through the interplay of perception and action. Understanding the affordances of extra-terrestrial environments is an especially fertile field of study for habitability.

the technology used to propel the rockets and the various stages of the flight as sections of the rocket detach have a long history. A capsule is still an architectural module for flights of short duration, attached to a rocket from which it separates, comprising a propulsion system and a cabin where astronauts are fastened to seats, with controls that they can still access despite their vastly reduced mobility.

Capsule habitats are autonomous, closed in on themselves by an external envelope, and therefore detached from but also linked to the structures that carry and propel them, as well as, potentially, to other habitats such as space stations with which they can dock. The capsules are compact and complete; their restraint systems constrain the astronauts' bodies from head to foot, fully united with the architectural bloc although the attachments can be adjusted during the various phases of a flight. Astronauts taking up position in the capsule's cabin are enveloped within a pressurised suit that encloses their body, supplies them with air and separates them from the capsule's architecture even as it connects them to it. Energy sources, a life-support cell and an infrastructure thus complement each other between the astronaut's body and the cabin, the cabin and the capsule, and the capsule and the rocket. The arrangement of these elements is precisely attuned to the concepts of the 'clip-on' and 'plug-in'[6] as elucidated in the radical architecture of Kisho Kurokawa or Archigram in the 1960s, designing 'machines for living-in' with parts and equipment fully connected together (Šenk, 2017). These technical arrangements hint at the fact that the habitability of these machines is constructed at the interface of two operations: the nesting of habitats one within another (pressurised suit inside cabin inside capsule inside rocket), and the attachments and detachments of their units (the inhabitants' bodies, habitation modules, infrastructures).

The line drawn by these attachments and detachments in the extra-terrestrial environment defines experimental coordinates for perceptions and actions, their measures being defined, in space research, by virtue of adaptations of bodies and subjects (combining physiology, psychology and ethology). Yet such studies must also be receptive to the exaptations made possible by these extra-terrestrial externalities (Andrieu, 2007), starting from the new sensorimotor planes that they open up. The space habitability laboratory could consider these estrangements of senses and bodies; but it could also comprehend how, within that environment, types of habitus as well

6   For Reyner Banham, the 'clip-on' in architecture is essentially about attaching an energy source to a life-support cell (an example being fitting a boat with an outboard motor) ('A Clip-on Architecture', Banham, 1965). But a life-support cell can also be 'clipped' to an infrastructure, corresponding to the concept of the 'plug-in' which was put to work by the Archigram collective. While the megastructure is permanent, the attachment of the cell is temporary and adjustable in number.

as cultural and social competencies and incompetencies are played out at the level of multilingual micro-communities based on relationships that are entirely divorced from distances, people and technological mediations: everything from telecommunications with Earth to proxemics in a confined space.

The relationships of attachment and detachment are still at the centre of metaphysical theories of extra-terrestrial subjects—whether one believes that any body removed from the Earth is still attached to it (Husserl, 1989) or that, under the effect of zero gravity, bodies are neither attached nor detached, but floating. Considered from the material plane of surfaces, these realities nevertheless lead us towards other conclusions: attachment to a surface is imperative for any Earthly body, since it creates the conditions for orientation, perception and action based on being grounded. And if, as the biologists believe, Earth's gravity is required for shaping life (Bizzarri, 2019), let us venture the hypothesis that attachments produced by virtue of technical objects in extra-terrestrial environments bring us back to the living rather than the existential.

On 9 August 2015, astronaut Scott Kelly posts a selfie on Twitter from the ISS. His face is half illuminated and half in shadow, and bathed in a strange, fluorescent pink light coming from a growth chamber in the background containing a romaine lettuce. The device is called Veggie (an abbreviation of Vegetable Production System), and was developed by the US company ORBITEC for NASA. It is a modular, transportable unit for growing plants, consisting of a root mat, a growth enclosure with a surface area of 0.17 m², and an LED lighting system. Veggie has been installed in the Columbus module since 2014. Most notably, Veggie is 'the first system designed for food production rather than plant experiments under microgravity' (Zabel *et al.*, 2016, p. 7).

This selfie, which rapidly went viral, found an echo in the photographs posted the following day on social networks showing astronauts Kelly, Lindgren, Yui, Kononenko, Padalka and Korniyenko tucking with obvious relish into the leaves of that

[Fig. 8] **Cosmonaut Viktor Savinykh observes an ornamental plant in the Malachite plant growth unit on board Salyut 6, 1981**

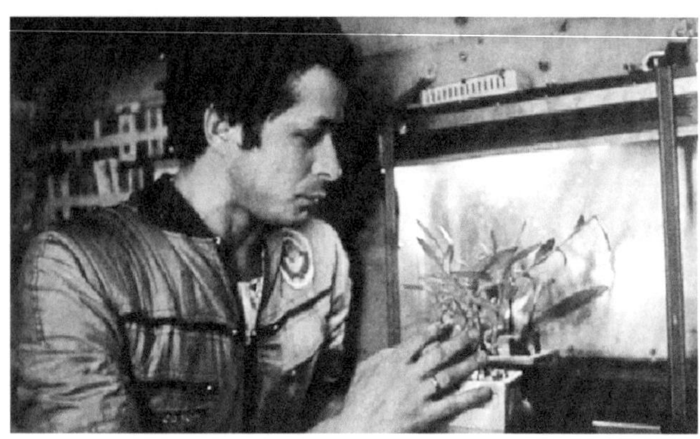

[Fig. 9] **Scott Kelly, Twitter post, 9 August 2015 (screenshot)**

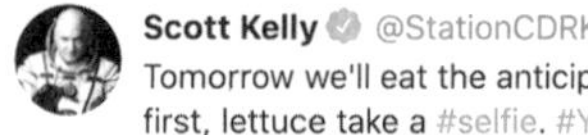

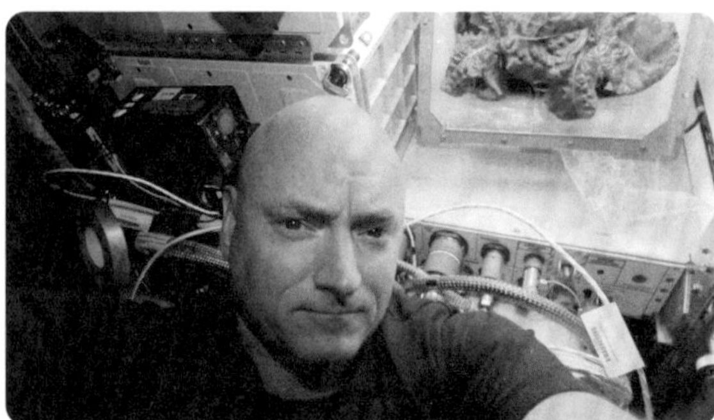

same lettuce—a sign that NASA had relaxed its strict standards with regard to food microbiology which had, until then, banned the consumption of food grown in space. Yet this was by no means a first in space botany: Russian cosmonauts had consumed onions grown in orbit on board Salyut 4 as far back as 1975 (Zabel *et al., op. cit.,* p.2).

Including plants, whether edible or not, in vital activity support systems is a huge challenge for space research, but one whose importance is emphasised by the texts of the early pioneers. Both Tsiolkovsky and Tsander commented on the need for agriculture in space. The first experiments begin with the earliest crewed flights: Vostok 1, which carries Gagarin into orbit, contains both fruit flies and packets of seeds.

Cosmonauts thus swiftly become laboratory technicians. Valery Bykovsky and Boris Yegorov conduct experiments on *tradescantia* (a herbaceous plant) in Vostok 5 (1963) and Voskhod 1 (1964) (Neichitailo and Mashinski, 1993, p. 21) respectively. But extended botanical experiments do not begin until 1971, when the first space stations go into orbit, enabling long-term stays. There are two separate strands of research. The first involves plant evolution in conditions of microgravity. The second, rooted in applied science, seeks to identify how to 'efficiently grow plants to provide a safe, nutritious and palatable food source for crews in space' (Massa *et al.,* 2016, p. 215–222) during a long mission. The two uses are precisely circumscribed: plants, whether as objects of study in botanical experiments or as fresh and tasty food, fall within a technical-scientific conception of habitability. In the selfie, the look on Kelly's face, inspired by the triumphalist rantings of the character of Mark Watney in *The Martian* when he successfully creates his vegetable garden on Mars, thus expresses his pride in a technical feat—getting a plant to grow in a hostile environment—and addresses it to his many followers.

However, plants can also be viewed from a third perspective. A comparison between Kelly's selfie—an image of communication—and this photograph of Viktor Savinykh, taken in 1981 on board the Salyut 6 station, can serve to show what we mean. In the second image, we see the cosmonaut gazing at a plant which turns out to be an orchid, even though it has no flowers. His eyes are directed not, as in Kelly's case, towards the viewer (or indeed towards himself, as the term 'selfie' might lead us to expect), but towards the plant. The cosmonaut reaches out gently to the orchid. A white, almost vaporous light has replaced the technological pink of the LEDs. The benevolent gaze turned on the plant, the bluish colour of the suit, the delicate hand with its tender gesture, and the relationship of scale between these two bodies, combine to locate this image within a visual tradition that has little in common with technical representations: it calls to mind images of the Virgin and Child, whereas Kelly's selfie is more reminiscent of hunters posing with their trophies. A sense of wonder replaces prowess.

Malachite, the piece of equipment which can be seen in the image, is the first ornamental plant device to have been taken on board a spacecraft, in 1979. Russian space research, particularly in the field of botany, soon noted the positive emotional effect of the presence of plants on board during long missions (Neichitailo and Masshinski, *op. cit.,* p.49). In the late 1970s, plants are sent into the orbit for the enjoyment of cosmonauts. And there is no shortage of testimonies to the importance of 'green friends', as Valery Ryumin (Salyut 6) called them (Bluth, 1987, p.294). In 1971, Viktor Patsayev described the plants on board Salyut 1 as animal companions. Valentin Lebedev, in his account of the mission on Salyut 7, makes frequent references to his interest in his 'garden' (Lebedev, 1990, p.405). Like the term 'malachite', which denotes a fine, intensely green stone often used for its decorative properties, Oasis, the name of Russia's first plant growth system in space, carries a metaphorical charge that extends beyond its technological uses.

It would be theoretically crude, and naive, to invoke the poets of space and engineers in the same breath, or to equate the pictorial tradition of high art with the vulgarity of shared images. The comparison is intended merely to confirm that in the emptiness of space, plants are companion species and denizens in their own right. The relationship that can be established with them cannot be reduced to a purely utilitarian function (which includes pleasure as much as the satisfaction of dietary needs), even if it implies it. The direction of Savinykh's gaze as he contemplates the orchid while Kelly turns his back on it merely hints that, as Sandra Häuplik-Meusburger puts it, 'Their future appears to extend beyond providing desirable add-ons, but as an essential habitability component' (Häuplik-Meusburger, 2011, p. 226). Or to quote Lebedev again: 'They are quite simply essential to human beings in space.' (Lebedev, *op. cit.*, p. 208)

In a number of photographs taken on board Salyut 6 in 1980, an image depicting the setting sun in tones of orange can be glimpsed in the background, against the cabin wall. Comparing various views taken at different times and with varying compositions of equipment, it becomes evident that the image is on a soft support. It is probably a small-format painting by an artist as yet unidentified—perhaps Galina Balashova, the architect of the Russian space programme, who painted a dozen or so watercolours of landscapes for Soyuz to 'brighten up the capsule' (Balashova, 2017, p. 53).

The incongruous presence of the image in this context is interesting in a number of respects. First of all, it suggests that surrounding oneself with images is a response to a pressing need. Many visual archives of space also offer—entirely unintentional—hints that images are a constant presence in orbiting spacecraft: while astronauts are laboratory technicians, they are also 'curators'

[Fig. 10] **Valery Ryumin, Bertsi Farkas and Valery Kubasov on board Salyut 6, 1980 We notice on the upper left corner of the picture, a painting that shows a sunset or sunrise, installed in the passenger compartment.**

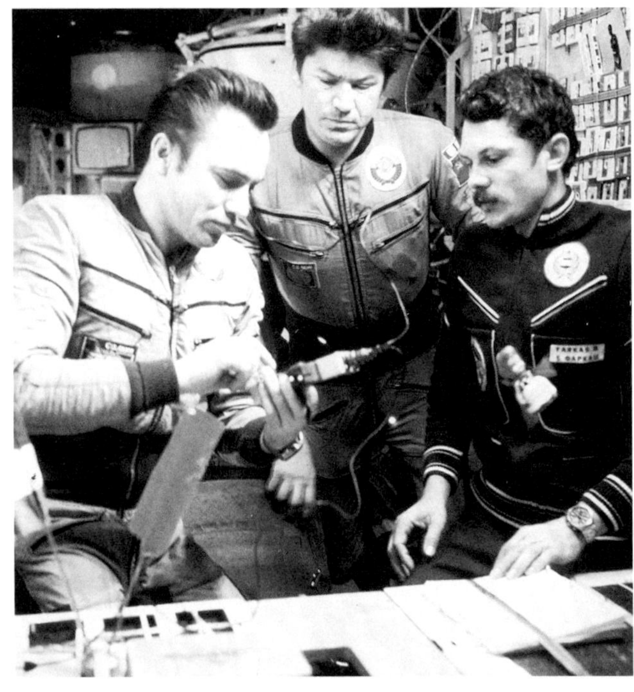

of their working and living environment. Aside from the obligatory succession of portraits of political leaders and key figures in the history of space exploration, from Brezhnev to Tsiolkovsky and Gagarin, departing astronauts take with them photographs of their loved ones, their children's drawings or images of their favourite landscapes. While some of these have a memory function (such as one showing the crew of the STS-51-L mission who died in the Challenger shuttle explosion that turns up again two years after the disaster hanging in the cabin of Discovery), others serve to create a sense of home away from home, a means of dreaming about or keeping in touch with Earth. These onboard images are thus manifestations of multiple intents and are embedded in a network of social relations. In a tech-heavy environment such as a space habitat, it is not uninteresting to find pockets of events that refuse to obey the laws of physics.

But this seemingly painted image is interesting for another reason. The various views of it that exist show it close to one, or sometimes two screens. At the same time, placed as it is and bearing this conventional representation of a celestial body, it could create the illusion of a window, in the manner of James Turrell's *Skyspaces*. The locations of this image thus invite us to reflect on the connections that exist in space habitats between image, viewing window and virtual window.

The importance of the presence of windows in space environments, despite the structural

[Fig. 11] **Virtual window function, deep space habitat unit (HDU-DSH) analog demonstration, 2012**

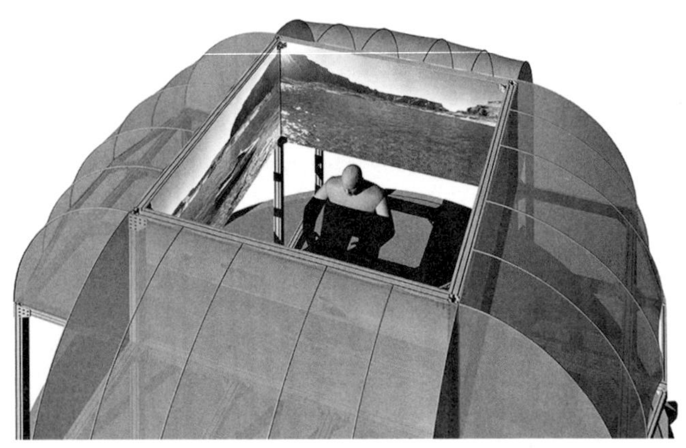

[Fig. 12] **Live video streams from simulated rover projected into HDU-DSH**

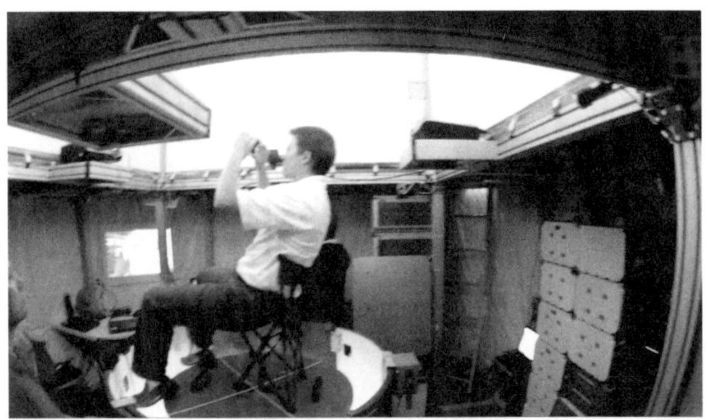

dangers it entails, has often been emphasised. The first American astronauts had to fight to get them (Wolfe, 1979); as did Raymond Loewy, who considered it 'inconceivable' that they should be absent from the interior of Skylab, the design of which he worked on as a habitability consultant. Today, astronauts spend much of their free time gazing out of windows at the Earth (Häuplik-Meusburger, 2011). The window is thus both a place in its own right and a space opening up on other—distant—spaces (Vogler, 2004).

Given how the need for them—and the attendant danger—increases with the length of time spent in space, research into virtual windows has recently developed in tandem with the work of engineers to enable the presence of physical openings in habitats. Space architect A. Scott Howe offers the following definition: 'Consisting of projections or images on virtual screens, Virtual Windows do not currently have the three-dimensionality of actual windows, but may eventually be configured to trick the eye and brain into inserting the person into the scene. Small spacecraft volumes can be artificially expanded to include the actual projected space outside, or pre-recorded environments.' Such windows thus combine a number of functions, expanding space (by means of *trompe-l'œil*) and allowing for immersion.

Devices of this nature do not belong purely to the realms of science fiction, from *Soylent Green* (1973) to *Sunshine* (2007) and *Ad Astra* (2019): they have been tested on various similar missions.

The Mars500 mission, for example, allowed for experiments with EARTH (Emotional Activities Related to Health), a technological system developed by Spanish researchers that uses virtual reality to reduce the stress induced by confinement. One of the modules, entitled 'Well-Being through Nature', involved immersing subjects in a simulation of natural environments (Botella, 2016). More recently, research conducted by NASA into the experimental prototype for a deep-space habitat unit (HDU-DSH) also looked into virtual windows aiming to offer an 'extended apparent volume' (Howe *et al.*, 2013, p.1) in restricted spaces requiring protection against radiation. In this specific case, the window-screens are multi-purpose, designed to serve as a pilot's cockpit, remote, robotic workstation, video conference support, or window all rolled into one. One of the applications envisaged involves projecting real-time images of outside space inside the habitat unit—a risky but ingenious exercise in truth and deception. In a different vein, consideration has been given to using growth units to create 'green windows' within space habitats, giving an illusion of depth using a system of sequencing spaces inspired by the Japanese technique of *shakkei* (which incorporates the background landscape into the composition of a garden) (Häuplik-Meusburger *et al.*, 2010).

The analogy between the window and the painted image has been well established since Alberti's treatise *De pictura*. But where do these new-style windows fit into this analogy? One answer can be found in Howe's expression, the 'extended apparent volume', which locates the virtual window firmly in the realm of *trompe-l'œil*, a pictorial genre in its own right. Virtual windows, then, are images, not windows.

Presenting them as 'positive technology to promote psychological wellbeing' (Baños *et al.*, 2012) cannot hoodwink us in the way that birds were fooled by Zeuxis's grapes. Astronauts' repeated calls for 'a real window (not a virtual window)' in a recent NASA report on conditions of habitability in deep space (NASA, 2019) or the testimony of participants in Mars500 commenting on the 'fastidious' (Urbina and Charles, 2014) dimension of these virtual applications also demonstrate that the inhabitants of space architectures cannot be convinced about windows by 'technological solutionism'. The presence of these images on the wall has undeniable psychological benefits, but it cannot replace the simple experience of a point of view: watching a sunset or a sunrise through a window or, like Alexei Leonov, directly from space.

[Fig. 13] **International Space Station Environmental Control and Life Support System Regenerative Environmental Control and Life Support System Diagram**

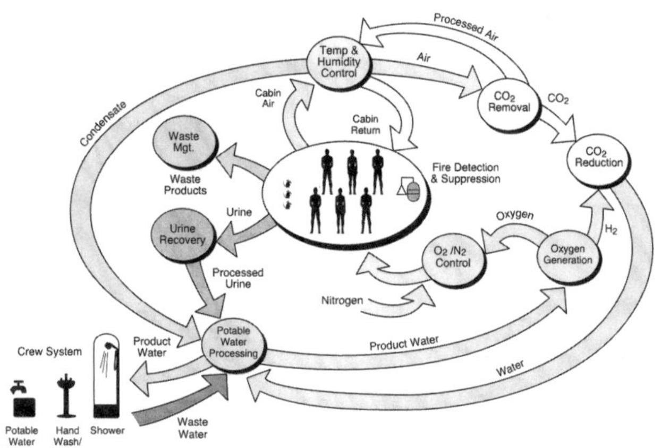

Many groups of researchers have emerged on the periphery of studies into space habitats. Based in the Netherlands, the International Association for the Advancement of Space Safety[7] investigates habitability in space from the perspective of safety, its technical systems and its design. The various elements that make up 'life support' in space habitats are central to their work, ensuring as they do the survival of those on board flights or spending time in space (Prokhorov, 2009). With astronauts now spending upwards of two weeks in flight or living in space stations, single-use life support systems supplied using material carried on board spacecraft are no longer viable. Complex systems, such as the Water Recovery System (WRS) (2008) and the Oxygen Generation System (OGS) (2007), have therefore been created to allow astronauts to spend extended periods in space as they have in,

7   The IAASS is a non-profit organisation established in 2004: http://iaass.space-safety.org/

[Fig. 14] **International Space Station Environmental Control and Life Support System Urine Processor Flight Experiment**

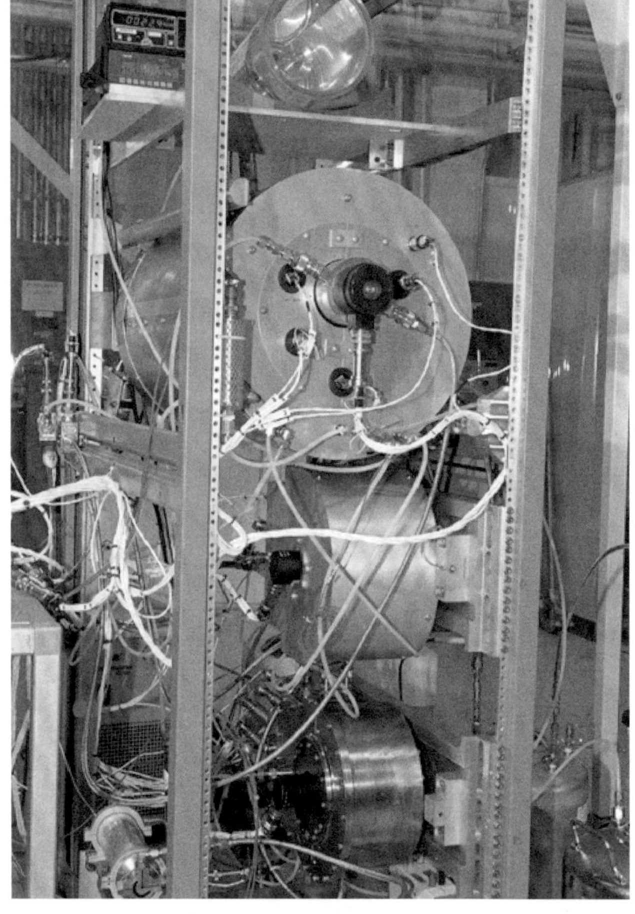

for example, the International Space Station, using regeneration and circulation of air and water to maintain an atmosphere within the habitats. These systems allow for regulation and control of humidity, filtering and recycling of the air breathed by those on board, and the treatment and purification of the astronauts' urine. The air and water systems are interlinked, because electrolysis of water is used to produce the oxygen that feeds the station's atmosphere, but also because carbon dioxide capture, combined with oxygen concentrators, generates hydrogen and allows water to be produced.

For guests in these extra-terrestrial habitats, the void and its absence of external resources signal a radical disconnect between an inside and an outside, which requires the highest degree of recycling in order to ensure the permanence of an environment; that, in turn, requires air and water to be preserved, and their density and the fluidity of their circulations to be maintained within a closed circuit.

Scientists studying and designing these systems approach questions of life support in terms of quantities, which are themselves linked to needs[8] and adaptations (Sgobba and Schlacht, 2018)—between metabolisms and materials, emissions and wastes, quotients and statistics. The balance of this technical and organic system requires each of its elements to work together in an alliance between living and artificial, physical and chemical; arrangements whereby human being, materials and technology are aligned interfaces that construct a closed and complete world. Nothing testifies more eloquently to the closed nature of its environment than the systematic nature of this recycling ecology, which ensures the permanence of the confined space, underscored as emphatically by its need for autarky and self-sufficiency as by the holistic perspective which pervades its arrangements and gives them coherence.

The category of 'human factors engineering' employed in space research by the Americans and Europeans sets out to understand how technological rationality can prevail in the quantitative evaluation of all the factors that go to make up the space habitat: noises, smells, food, sleep, hygiene, communication, light, ergonomics, human-machine interfaces, physiological and psychological countermeasures, and so on. In this approach, the habitable area becomes a residual volume defined by the space taken up by the technical

8   These needs are divided into two categories: basic and advanced, drawing a distinction between physiological necessities and psychological accomplishments.A system that combines quantification and gradation runs from the most basic need to the highest.
The satisfaction of a basic need, such as a quantity of food for a given body, is at the bottom of the scale; but that satisfaction is a precondition for meeting a higher need—one which, being higher, is also rarer—such as recognition from one's peers.
This pyramid is known as Maslow's hierarchy of needs: a tool that is chiefly designed to optimise individual productivity and is widely used in aerospace studies; as it moves from the physiological to the psychological, it subjects social behaviour to the same rules as biological equilibrium.

equipment. Such technical realism entails dividing up and locating zones of habitability according to activities relating to needs and productivity (eating, sleeping, working, etc.) (Song Lockard, Häuplik-Meusburger).

Ever since the early 1960s, the development of crewed flight programmes has combined two scientific objectives: exploring celestial objects and conducting multidisciplinary experiments—in physics, astronomy and biology, some of them relating to the inhabitants themselves (NASA, 1987). The concept of the orbiting laboratory is a response to these scientific objectives and the space station—a kind of intermediary point between the Earth and distant planets—is the place where explorations are conceived but also where experiments into living conditions take place.

A laboratory is a tool in which phenomena are produced and amplified with degrees of intensity that enable their variables and thresholds to be studied. Taken together, the extreme conditions of the extra-terrestrial environment—a combination of confinement and microgravity—amplify those of life on Earth but also enable us to understand its values.

The inhabitants of orbiting space stations thus have a dual affiliation with the laboratory space: as scientists conducting experiments and making observations in a zero-gravity context from various disciplines; and as guinea pigs placed in living conditions that themselves have experimental value, their behaviour and bodies being observed and described, over time, by a large number of observation instruments and measuring devices. Yet the laboratory is not simply an element aboard a structure located in orbit: it can also be viewed as an inverse model for space habitats, inasmuch as they construct scale models of worlds in accordance with the laws of scientific realism and the various disciplines that they cover—from engineering and ergonomics to psychology.

As the closed circuit of the life support systems in the extra-terrestrial laboratory reminds us, its inhabitants, be they human, animal or vegetable, all share the same state of existence, namely captivity. Of course, that captive state acts on their organisms and changes their behaviour, be it individual, collective or social. But what is the ecological validity of the experiment? In other words, what environment other than that of the orbiting laboratory could it be applied to? As the point at which all space habitabilities converge, captivity is a condition of the terrestrial being that can be generalised to any extra-terrestrial environment; but also, conversely, it is a glimpse of the future for terrestrial beings experiencing extreme conditions—the kind of which climate change is an alarming portent.

FLYING CITIES: LEAVING EARTH, AND COMING BACK

The motif of the flying city appears in literature long before the first space stations are sent into orbit. But in the 20th century, such cities are conceived along two distinct, concurrent lines. The first is in Russia in the years 1910–1920, the second in the United States between 1965 and 1980. Unsurprisingly, they represent neither the same vision of living in space nor the same conception of the city.

In Russia, the Suprematist reconstruction of the world embraces the urban environment, via planning, but also the habitat, as taken up by the Cosmism of Fedorov and, of course, Tsiolkovsky. Malevich speaks of 'leaving Earth' and describes the Suprematist work to come in the form of a satellite located between Earth and the Moon (Malevich, 1985). El Lissitzky translates his aspirations into volumes 'floating in space' (Lissitzky, 1992, p. 327), while Klutsis conceives dynamic cities that he places within spherical, planet-like shapes. But it is Georgy Krutikov who, for his concluding

[Fig. 15] **Georgy Krutikov, *The City of the Future,* perspective view. Diploma project, VKhUTEIN, Moscow, 1928**

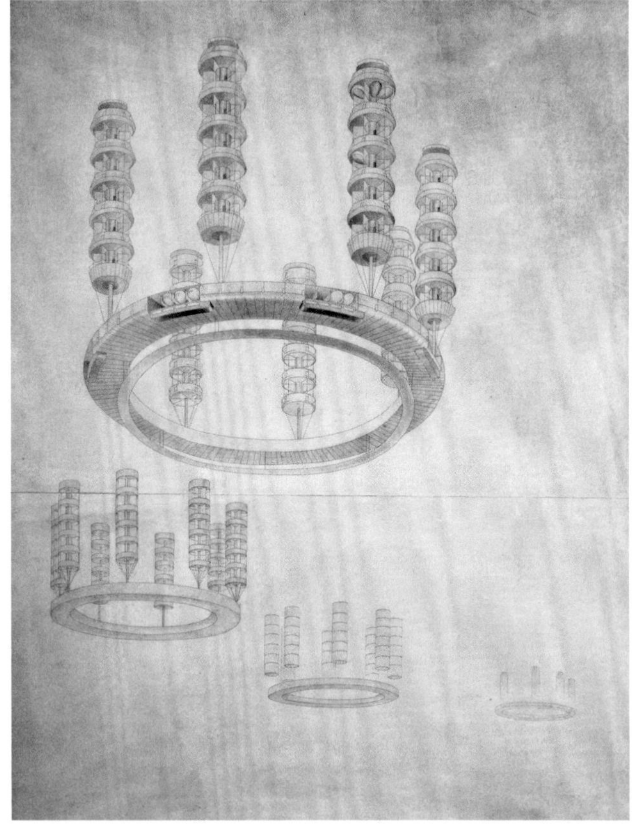

diploma project at VKhUTEIN in 1928, develops the first project for a flying city. Starting out from the idea that 'the plans of cities, the majority of them lifeless and uncomfortable' would gain by becoming 'mobile structures' (Khan-Magomedov, 1979, p. 241-247), he sets out to reflect on cities detached from the ground. These 'cities of the future', as he calls them, make up different types of habitat. Consisting of two conjoined parts—one industrial and on the ground, the other residential and in the air—they float without being mobile.

In America, meanwhile, a technological and scientific approach to the city takes hold after the Second World War. Technology transfers from space to civil applications, which gather pace in the 1960s (Light, 2003; Scharmen, 2019), are also fed by a cybernetic credo which sees the space habitat and the city as two systems that can be managed scientifically via the collection and computer processing of data and the management of flows. By the late 1960s, the Department of Housing and Urban Development (HUD) has begun working with NASA. In 1967, Volta Torrey, a NASA researcher temporarily seconded to HUD, publishes *Science and the city,* a report summarising the results of recent encounters between specialists in urban planning. This highly eloquent text opens with a comparison of the city and the spacecraft, and concludes by bringing together two grand objectives: the Moon and the American City. It is imbued throughout with a scientific and technological vision that extols the virtues of innovation,

[Fig. 16] **Rick Guidice, Cutaway View
of a Toroidal Colony, 1975 (detail)**

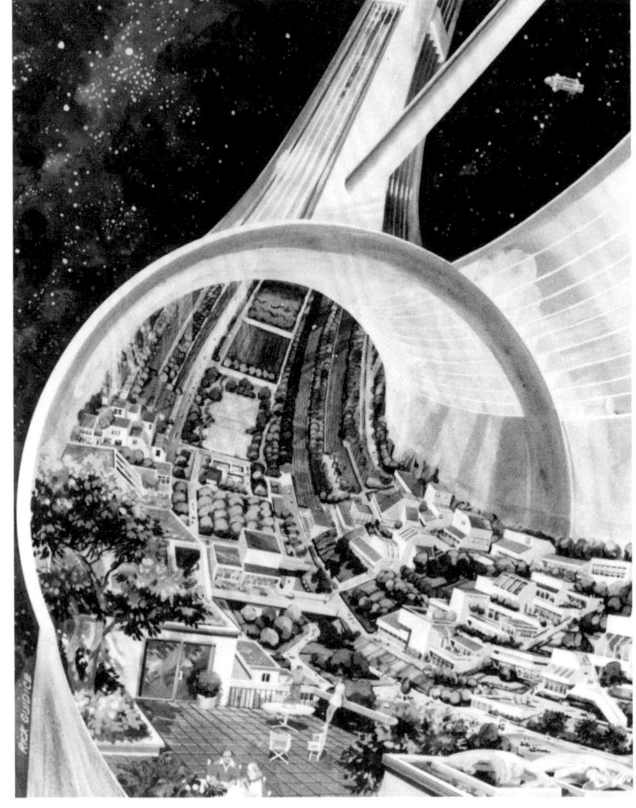

and approaches each phenomenon through the prism of the 'system' and 'sub-system'. In summer 1969, shortly after the success of the Apollo mission, Operation Breakthrough is launched, promising to research and develop a mass-produced, standardised and prefabricated habitat, with 35 engineers and technicians from NASA contributing their expertise (Mahler, 2019). Space technologies covering everything from waste management and electricity production and distribution to the regulation of environments and systems engineering soon find applications in the domestic sphere back on Earth. Indeed, it is that convergence of urban planning and space, with a dash of cybernetics, that inspires the physicist Gerard O'Neill's reflections on orbiting space colonies in the early 1970s, in which he questions the idea that 'the surface of a planet [is] really the right place' (Brand, 1977) to install them.

These two historical lineages embody two visions of the city and the habitat. On one side is the city-planet imagined and designed in response to (supposed) human aspirations to what Krutikov called an 'extension of the horizon', a fierce desire to leave Earth; and on the other a city-machine, conceived pragmatically in terms of problem solving (tackling housing shortages or urban riots) and so on, based on the technological capacities available to process information and construct or manage energy or environmental systems. In many respects, these two visions of the city dictate the design of the orbiting space stations that come into being on either side of the Iron Curtain in the early 1970s: as location for an extra-terrestrial experiment on the one hand, and demonstration of technological and economic might on the other.

In December 1971, a project by the Italian group Superstudio entitled 'Twelve Cautionary Tales for Christmas: Premonitions of the Mystical Rebirth of Urbanism' is published in *Architectural Digest*. It presents twelve projects for 'ideal cities' that draw inspiration from the principles of Modernism but extrapolate them and subject them to fierce criticism. The fourth is the 'spaceship city', a huge red wheel 50 metres in diameter with a crew of 156 which 'for centuries has been following a precise route towards a planet thousands of light-years away'. Here, the conquest of space is itself critiqued along with the habitat-machines that it creates, which are parodied to the extreme in the organisation of 160 cabins divided up by age, and in a strictly functionalist principle of habitability that sees those on board 'enveloped in the cables and pipelines which regulate their existence' and piloted by a central electronic brain. If it is a city at all, it is, literally, a dormitory city and machine city. The observation contained in the text, that one can design this wheel, in a parody of von Braun's research, as a city 'independently of its physical and demographical dimensions' nevertheless poses a central question, namely: what defines a city? The size of its population? Its density? The technical sophistication of the systems that sustain its existence?

Salyut 1 is sent into orbit in April 1971, and two months later a crew of three cosmonauts arrives (after the failure of a first mission). Skylab is launched in May 1973, and the first mission to the station with astronauts on board sets off one month later. It, too, carries a crew of three. Since this pioneering age, the stations have not really been populated. Mir, launched in 1986 and active until 2001, was designed to accommodate three permanent residents, the ISS six. Those numbers may increase slightly during visits, but they rarely exceed ten or so. In comparison with the extravagant projects that have punctuated the history of astronautics and science fiction, the orbiting space stations that have actually been built are more akin to space hamlets.

Two concepts have emerged within scientific research into extra-terrestrial habitability: the 'habitable zone' and the 'habitable planet'. In the late 19th century, a 'habitable zone' meant terrestrial climate conditions under which human life and the life of other vegetable and animal species could develop (Messeri, 2016). When it was transposed into astronomical research, replacing the grand narrative of the plurality of worlds, the concept of the 'habitable zone' stabilised, coming to denote areas in which celestial bodies are located at a distance where the energy supplied by the radiation from a star allows them to maintain a surface temperature compatible with the presence of water in a liquid state. The commonest representation of these zones has been formalised into a band delimited by the orbits of Venus and Mars in the solar system (Kihm, 2019, p. 167-170).

When it comes to the location of exoplanets, 'habitable zones' are populated with 'habitable planets'. Extra-terrestrial habitabilities, meanwhile, have been examined by abandoning the criteria of terrestrial habitability in favour of analogues produced by the many disciplines involved in space research. In biology, for example, these suggest adopting a hydrocentric perspective, identifying the presence of water as a condition precedent for the development of extra-terrestrial life forms; in physics, they involve studying planets linked to their stars where an equivalence exists as between the Earth and the Sun; in geology, they investigate terrestrial sites defined as analogues of extra-terrestrial sites.

The understanding of Mars and its exploration on the basis of a terrestrial model is a prime example of this (Heams, 2019). The investigations carried out by the Curiosity (2012–) and ExoMars (planned for 2022) missions into the traces of cellular life left by micro-organisms transform Mars into a fossil Earth, while the many terrestrial sites identified as analogues of the Martian surface for the purpose of conducting experiments and simulations of life envisage the red planet as a future colony (from the Mars Desert Research Station in Utah to the Hawaii Space Exploration Analog and Simulation IV) (Messeri, 2014).

Placed at the two ends of a temporal line linking a distant past to an uncertain future, these experiments reveal a practical advantage of the analogue in science: it makes what is outside us more familiar. Analogies are thus made not only to reduce the distances between remote objects but also to establish continuities between

[Fig. 17] Viking 1, July 20, 1976,
First photograph taken from the
surface of Mars

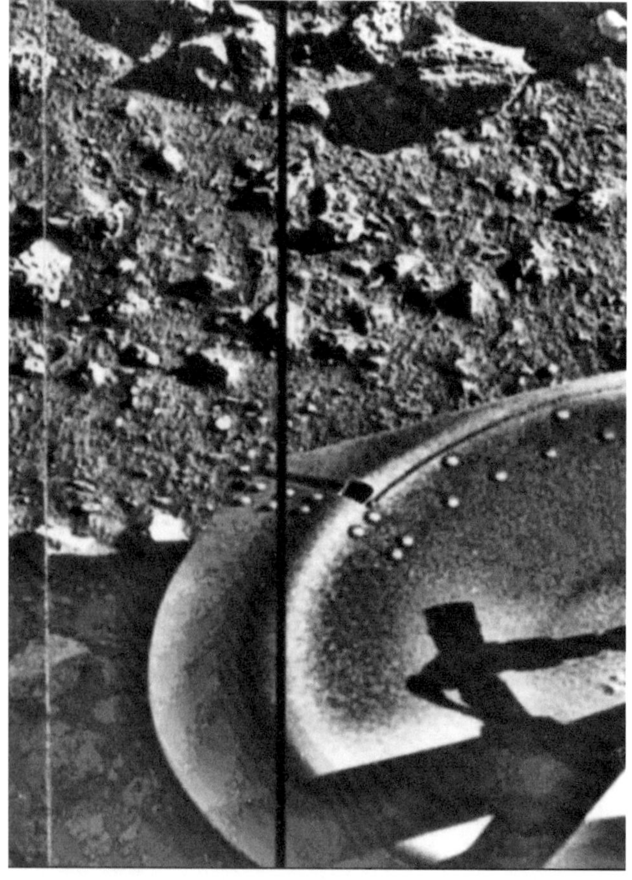

discontinuous realities. Intermediate in the literal sense, the act of identifying an analogue involves a relocation of scientific knowledge, both theoretical and practical; examples include applying a concept of terrestrial life (cellular, hydrocentric) to the quest for extra-terrestrial life or transposing Martian geology to Earth geology for the purpose of simulations and life experiments.

While the analogue produces short-circuits between the terrestrial and the extra-terrestrial, it remains to be seen what the effects will be on science itself. Three points can be identified in respect of extra-terrestrial habitability. First, a distinction should be made between analogies that are speculative or applied, functional or formal. Those that are used to formulate a hypothesis in order to grasp an unknown phenomenon—for example when theorists of synthetic evolution attempt to delineate the forms of a living extra-terrestrial entity—are speculative (Vakoch, 2014). 'Applied analogies' are obtained by transposing a theoretical model, be it from physics, geology or biology, from one object to another, one example being the terrestrial life form adopted as a model for extra-terrestrial life. Functional analogies are based on values that are deemed to be sufficiently common for the properties of one place to be mapped onto another—one example being the equivalences posited between the aquatic and the Martian (or lunar) environments when conducting experiments in reduced gravity, or between confinement on Earth and extra-terrestrial

[Fig. 18] **Kepler-186f**

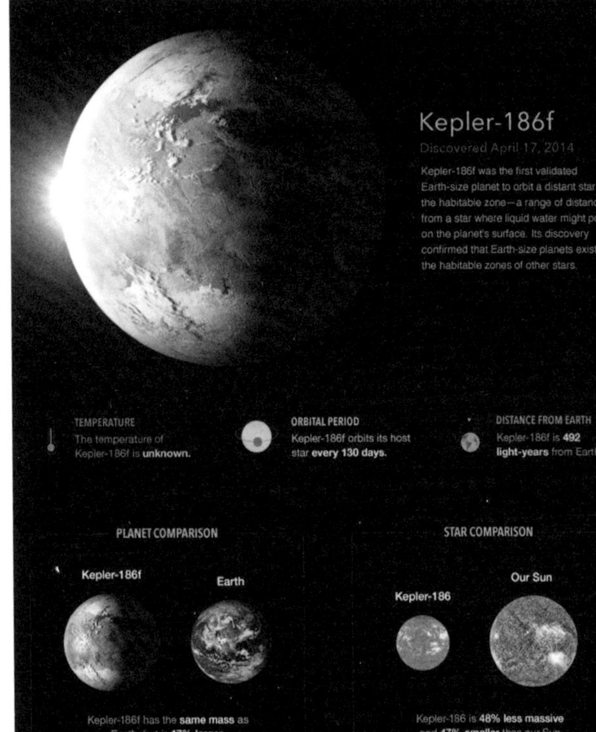

confinement when carrying out psychological experiments (Tafforin, 2015). Formal analogies are based on similarities in qualities of appearance between one object and another; rarely serving to create structure in the field of scientific research, they can be regarded as effects of the three categories of analogies cited earlier.

The second point describes the changes made to knowledge by relocating it. One key location that could be useful for this enquiry—since it is situated at the crossroads of these new orientations for knowledge, and facilitates these crossovers between the terrestrial and the extra-terrestrial—is the laboratory. When extended to a cosmos populated with tools for visualising and measuring—probes, telescopes, satellites and rovers—the laboratory conducts its study of extra-terrestrial habitability on the basis of quantitative physical, chemical or geological data obtained from faraway worlds. But the laboratory is also the place on Earth where models of extra-terrestrial worlds are made and experiments with living in entirely different physical, chemical or geological conditions are verified. Located midway between the terrestrial and the extra-terrestrial, the laboratory is thus the place where the analogue extensions of habitability are conceived.

The last point would be to consider an 'applied analogy' whose importance has historically created structure for studies of habitability. The mostly functionalist approaches to space habitability ultimately unite celestial bodies and organic bodies around a common criterion: 'need', transposed to material, physiological or psychological planes and linking the resources available at planetary level (Lunine, 2013) to the needs of the subjects who travel and live there. This quantitative approach to habitability, which involves managing an environment and its supposed populations, plays out in the extra-terrestrial domain a scene from a capitalist drama that gives every cause for concern, since it is the vehicle of a new universalism encouraged by the privatisation of outer space and the liberal exploitation of a vacuum that, this time round, is of the legal variety.

Bibliography

Tactile experience: the glove

Abts, K. J., 'Mechanical counter pressure glove for spacesuit,' U.S. Patent (6 000 059), 14 December 1999

Bach-y-Rita, P., Webster, J. G. and Tompkins, W. J., 'Sensory Substitution for Space Gloves and for Space Robots,' in *Proceedings of the Workshop on Space Telerobotics*, vol. 2, (ed. G. Rodriguez), NASA / Jet Propulsion Laboratory (California Institute of Technology), 1987

Malafouris, L., *How Things Shape the Mind: A Theory of Material Engagement*, Cambridge MA / London, MIT Press, 2013

Marinetti, F., 'Le tactilisme: manifeste futuriste,' in *Comoedia*, January 1921

Talvi, A., 'Sartorial Thoughts on Tailoring Spacesuits,' in *Moving to Mars, Design for the Red Planet* (ed. J. McGuirk, A. Nahum and E. Watson), London, The Design Museum Publishing, 2019

The diving suit as mobile habitat

Clynes, M. E. and Kline, N. S., 'Cyborgs and Space,' in *Journal of Astronautics*, September 1960

Colombetti, G., 'Enaction, Sense-Making and Emotion,' in *Enaction: Toward a New Paradigm for Cognitive Science* (ed. J. Stewart, O. Gapenne, E. A. Di Paolo), Cambridge, MA / London, MIT Press (Bradford Books), 2010

Jenkins, D. R., *Dressing for Altitude: U.S. Aviation Pressure Suits—Wiley Post to Space Shuttle*, Washington DC, National Aeronautics and Space Administration (NASA SP [Series]), 2012

Marlier, T. and Mouriaux, P.-M., *Profession astronaute*, Paris, Paulsen / Arte Editions, 2017

Monchaux, N. de, *Spacesuits: Fashioning Apollo*, Cambridge, MA, MIT Press, 2011

Shepard, L. F. *et al.*, 'Space suit,' U.S. Patent (3 751 727), 14 August 1973

Young, A. and Avino, M., *Spacesuits, The Smithsonian National Air and Space Museum Collection*, Washington DC, Smithsonian National Air and Space Museum / Brooklyn NY, powerHouse Books, 2009

Zhang, C., Zadtootaghaj, S., Hoel, A. S. and Perkis, A., 'How Long is Long Enough to Induce Immersion? Comparing the

Immersiveness of Three Variations of Spatial Immersion,' Conference Paper, 10th International Conference on Quality of Multimedia Experience (QoMEX 2018), Sardinia, 29 May–1 June 2018

Missile, launcher, icon, habitat

Ananoff, A., *L'Astronautique*, Paris, Fayard, 1950

Bartholeyns, G., 'Espaces du V2,' in *Espaces* no. 17, Paris, Observatoire de l'Espace / CNES, February 2019

Braun, W. von, 'Crossing the Last Frontier,' in *Collier's,* 22 March 1952

Clarke, A. C., 'Letter to the editors,' in *Wireless World*, February 1945

Fontana, L. 'Pourquoi je suis spatialiste,' 1952, in *Écrits de Lucio Fontana, Manifestes, textes, entretiens* (ed. V. Da Costa), Les Presses du réel, 2013

Häuplik-Meusburger, S., *Architecture for Astronauts: An Activity-based Approach*, Vienna, Springer, 2011

Le Maner, Y., 'Histoire, mémoire, patrimoine spatial: le cas du V2,' in *Les représentations de l'espace* (ed. G. Azoulay), Paris, Observatoire de l'espace, CNES, 2007

Macauley, W. R., 'Crafting the Future: Envisioning Space Exploration in Post-war Britain,' in *History and Technology* (28) 3, 2012

McCurdy, H., *Space and the American Imagination*, Baltimore, Johns Hopkins University Press, 2011

Neufeld, M. J., *The Rocket and the Reich: Peenemünde and the Coming of the Ballistic Missile Era*, London, Simon and Schuster, 1994

Neufeld, M. J., *Von Braun. Dreamer of Space, Engineer of War*, New York, Vintage Books, 2008

Newell, C. L., *Destined for the Stars*, Pittsburgh, University of Pittsburgh Press, 2019

Rambert, F. (ed.), *Un bâtiment, combien de vies?: La transformation comme acte de création*, Milan and Paris, Silvana Editoriale and Cité de l'architecture et du patrimoine, 2015

Song Lockard, E., 'From Hostile to Hospitable: Changing Perceptions of the Space Environment,' 45th International Conference on Environmental Systems, 12–16 July 2015, Bellevue, Washington, ICES–2015–156

Winter, F. H., *Rockets into Space*, Harvard University Press, 1993

Attachment and the living

Andrieu, B., 'L'externalité du corps cérébré: épistémologie de la constitution interactive du corps et du monde,' in *Philosophia Scientiæ*, 11–1, Paris, Éditions Kimé, 2007

Bizzarri, M., 'Why Earth Gravity is Required for Shaping Life,' in *LINKs Series no. 4* (ed. L.-J. Lestocart), dossier 'Espace habité' (coordinated by C. Kihm), 2019, http://links-series.com/wp-content/uploads/2019/11/Why-earth-gravity-is-required-for-shaping-life.pdf

Husserl, E., *La Terre ne se meut pas*, Paris, Minuit, 1989

Šenk, P., *Capsules, Typology of Other Architecture*, London, Routledge, 2017

Sgobba, T. and Schlacht, I. L., 'Habitability and Habitat Design,' in *Space Safety and Human Performance* (ed. B. Kanki, J.-F. Clervoy and G. Sandal), Butterworth-Heinemann, 2018

The company of plants

Bluth, M. H., *Soviet Space Stations as Analogs*, Washington, NASA ,1987

Casado, J., 'Agriculture in Space,' in *Spaceflight—The Magazine of Astronautics and Outer Space* 48 (5), 2006

Granjou, C. and Walker, J., 'MELiSSA la biosphère minimale: composter dans l'espace,' blog post (7 September 2018), in *Humanités spatiales*, http://humanites-spatiales.fr/melissa-la-biosphere-minimale-composter-dans-lespace/

Häuplik-Meusburger, S., *Architecture for Astronauts: An Activity-based Approach*, Vienna, Springer, 2011

Häuplik-Meusburger, S., Peldszus, R. and Holzgethan, V., 'Greenhouse Design Integration Benefits for Extended Spaceflight,' in *Acta Astronautica* 68, 2011

Haüplik-Meusburger, S., Paterson, C., Schubert, D. and Zabel, P., 'Greenhouses and their Humanizing Synergies,' in *Acta Astronautica* 96, 2014

Lebedev, V., *Diary of a Cosmonaut: 211 Days in Space*, New York, Bantam Books, 1990

Massa, G. D., Wheeler, R. M., Morrow, R. C., Levine, H. G., 'Growth Chambers on the International Space Station for Large Plants,' in *Acta Horticulturae*, 1134, 2016

Neichitailo, G. S. and Mashinski, A. L., *Space Biology: Studies at Orbital Stations*, Moscow, Mir Publishing, 1993

Zabel, P., Bamsey, M., Schubert, D., Tajmar, M., 'Review and Analysis of Over 40 Years of Space Plant Growth Systems,' in *Life Sciences in Space Research*, vol. 10, August 2016

The onboard image and the window

Balashova, G., 'Des espaces aménagés,' interview with Gérard Azoulay, in *artpress 2* no. 44, 2017

Baños, R. M., Botella, C. and Alcañiz, M., '"Earth of Well-being": a Positive Technology to Promote Psychological Well-being,' international symposium ('Mars–500' project), Moscow, 2012

Botella, C., Baños, R. M., Etchemendy, E., García-Palaciosa, A. and Alcañiz, M., 'Psychological Countermeasures in Manned Space Missions: "EARTH" system for the Mars–500 project,' in *Computers in Human Behavior* 55, 2016

'Deep Space Habitability Design Guidelines Based on the NASA NextSTEP Phase 2 Ground Test Program', [NASA/TP–2020–220505], 2019

Häuplik-Meusburger, S., *Architecture for Astronauts: An Activity-based Approach*, Vienna, Springer, 2011

Häuplik-Meusburger, S., Peldszus, R. and Holzgethan, V., 'Greenhouse Design Integration Benefits for Extended Spaceflight,' in *Acta Astronautica 68*, 2010

Howe, S. A., Howard, R. L., Moore, N., Amoroso, M., 'Designing for Virtual Windows in a Deep Space Habitat,' International Conference on Environmental Systems (ICES), Vail, CO, July 2013

Leonov, A., 'An Artist in Space,' in *In the Stream of Stars*, New York, Workman Publishing, 1990

Morozov, E., *To Save Everything, Click Here: The Folly of Technological Solutionism*, New York, PublicAffairs Books, 2013

Urbina, D. A. and Charles, R., 'Symposium Keynote: Enduring the Isolation of Interplanetary Travel: A Personal Account of the Mars–500 Mission,' in *Acta Astronautica 93*, 2014

Vogler, A. and Jørgensen, J., 'Windows to the World—Doors to Space—A Reflection on the Psychology and Anthropology of Space Architecture,' Space: Science, Technology and the

Arts (7th Workshop on Space and the Arts), ESA/ESTEC, Noordwijk, NL, 18–21 May 2004

Wolfe, T., *The Right Stuff*, New York, Farrar, Straus and Giroux, 1979

The closed circuit and captivity

Allahdadi, F., Rongier, I., Wilde, P. and Sgobba, T. (ed.), *Safety Design for Space Operations*, Butterworth-Heinemann, 2013

Häuplik-Meusburger, S., *Architecture for Astronauts: An Activity-based Approach*, Vienna, Springer, 2011

Prokhorov, K. S., 'Life Support Systems Safety,' in *Safety Design for Space Systems* (ed. G. Eugene Musgrave, A.M. Larsen and T. Sgobba), Butterworth-Heinemann / Elsevier, 2009

'Space Station Habitability and Function: Architectural Research,' in *Space Station Human Factors Research Review*, vol. 3, [NASA Technical Reports Server (NTRS) 19880010499], 1987

Song Lockard, E., 'From Hostile to Hospitable: Changing Perceptions of the Space Environment,' in *LINKs Series no. °4*, dossier 'Habitabilités,' http://links-series.com/

wp-content/uploads/2019/11/ From-Hostile-to-Hospitable.pdf

Flying cities: leaving Earth, and coming back

Brand, S., 'Is the Surface of a Planet Really the Right Place for an Expanding Technological Civilization?,' interview with Gerard O'Neill, in *Space Colonies* (ed. S. Brand), A Co-Evolution Book, Whole Earth Catalogue/Penguin, 1977

Khan-Magomedov, S. O., 'Georgij Krutikov: projet de ville volante,' *Cahiers du Musée national d'art moderne*, Paris, 1979

Glaeser, L., 'Architectural Studies for a Space Habitat (1975), in *Space Manufacturing Facilities*, New York, AIAA, 1977

Johnson, J. D. and Holbrow, C. (ed.), *Space Settlements, A Design Study*, NASA SP–413, 1977

Light, J. S., *From Warfare to Welfare, Defense Intellectuals and Urban Problems in Cold War America*, Johns Hopkins University Press, 2003

Lissitzky, E., 'Suprematism in World Reconstruction,' in *El Lissitzky: Life, Letters, Texts / Sophie Lissitzky-Küppers*, London, Thames & Hudson, 1992

Maher, N. M., *Apollo in the Age of Aquarius*, Harvard University Press, 2019

Malevitch, K., *Le Suprématisme: 34 dessins*, Paris, Chêne, 1985

Mumford, L., 'Utopia, the City and the Machine,' in *Daedalus*, vol. 94, no. 2, 'Utopia,' spring 1965

O' Neill, G., *The High Frontier, Human Colonies in Space*, New York, Toronto and London, Bantam Books, 1977

Scharmen, F., *Space Settlements*, Columbia University Press, 2019

Superstudio, 'Twelve Cautionary Tales for Christmas: Premonitions of the Mystical Rebirth of Urbanism,' in *Architectural Digest*, December 1971

Planetary analogies

Heams, T., *Infravies. Le vivant sans frontières*, Paris, Le Seuil, Science ouverte collection, 2019

Kihm, C., 'Habitabilités extra-terrestres, ou comment quitter la Terre?,' in *LINKs Series*, no. 1–2, dossier 'Virtuel, Biologie' (ed. L.-J. Lestocart), 2019, http://links-series.com/ wp-content/uploads/2019/10/ Habitabilit%C3%A9s-extraterrestres-ou-comment-quitter-la-Terre.pdf

Lunine, J. I., *Earth. Evolution of a Habitable World*, 2nd edition, Cornell University, Cambridge University Press, 2013

Messeri, L., 'Earth as Analog: The Disciplinary Debate and Astronaut Training that Took Geology to the Moon,' in *Astropolitics: The International Journal of Space Politics & Policy*, University of Virginia, Charlottesville, VA, 2014

Messeri, L., *Placing Outer Space. An Earthly Ethnography of Other Worlds*, Durham and London, Duke University Press, 2016

Tafforin, C., 'Confinement vs. Isolation as Analogue Environments for Mars Missions from a Human Ethology Viewpoint,' in *Aerospace Medicine and Human Performance*, vol. 86, no. 2, February 2015

Vakoch, D. A., 'The Evolution of Extraterrestrials. The Evolutionary Synthesis and Estimates of the Prevalence of Intelligence Beyond Earth,' in *Archaeology, Anthropology, and Interstellar Communication* (ed. D. A. Vakoch), NASA History Program Office, Washington, 2014

Colophon

HEAD – Publishing, 2021

Texts published under free license CC BY–SA

Title: *Ways to leave Earth* (original title: *Comment quitter la Terre?*) ·

Authors: Christophe Kihm, Jill Gasparina, Anne-Lyse Renon

Manifestes collection edited by Julie Enckell Julliard and Anthony Masure

Editorial coordinator: Sylvain Menétrey

Translation: Geoffrey Spearing

Proofreading: Stephanie O'Dea

Correctorat : Martine Passelaigue

Manifestes collection designed by Dimitri Broquard

Fonts: ABC Whyte (Dinamo, 2019), Lyon Text (Commercial Type, 2009)

Printed by Artgraphic Cavin SA

Ways to Leave Earth is published as part of the 'Inhabiting the Extra-terrestrial Space' research project headed by Christophe Kihm at HEAD – Genève in partnership with the Space Observatory (CNES, Paris) and supported by the Swiss National Science Foundation (SNFS project #178992, 2018–2022).

ISBN: 978-2-940510-49-8

Legal deposit: March 2021

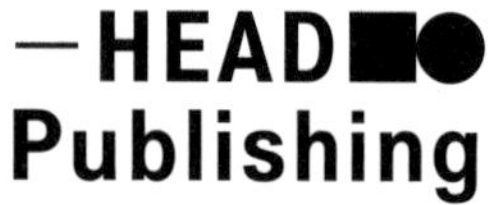

Images credits

[Fig. 1.] © VPL Research Inc.,
    CNES Archives
[Fig. 2.] © VPL Research Inc.,
    CNES Archives
[Fig. 3.] CNES Archives
[Fig. 4.] © Smithsonian
Institution
[Fig. 5.] Elon Musk Twitter
    Post, 11.01.2019
[Fig. 6.] © NASA
[Fig. 7.] Private collection, Paris
[Fig. 8.] © Roscosmos
[Fig. 9.] Scott Kelly Twitter
    Post, 09.08.2015
[Fig. 10.] © Roscosmos
[Fig. 11.] © NASA
[Fig. 12.] © NASA
[Fig. 13.] © NASA
[Fig. 14.] © NASA
[Fig. 15.] Courtesy A.V. Shusev
    Architecture Museum,
    Moscow
[Fig. 16.] © NASA Ames Center
[Fig. 17.] © NASA
[Fig. 18.] © NASA. Ames.
    JPL-Caltech

Jill Gasparina is art critic, freelance exhibition curator and lecturer at HEAD—Genève. After studying at the École normale supérieure in Lyon and obtaining a Master's degree in modern literature, she turned to studying the visual arts, writing criticism and teaching at art school. She was director of the La Salle de Bains art centre in Lyon from 2009 to 2013, and was then in charge of visual arts programming at Confort Moderne (Poitiers) from 2015 to 2017. Her research focuses in particular on technological imaginaries in art and the phenomena of mass production in pop culture. She is a researcher at HEAD—Genève working on the SNSF project 'Inhabiting the Extra-terrestrial Space.'

Christophe Kihm is professor at HEAD—Genève, as well as a freelance critic and exhibition curator. His research has principally focused on the artistic practices of the archive, teaching methods in the teaching of art, and the action arts. More recently, starting from ethology and on the fringes of anthropology, he has become interested in ways of living, interspecies conflicts and interworlds. On behalf of HEAD, he was included in the ArTeC research project 'Politique de la distraction' (2017–2019) in partnership with ESTCA (University of Paris 8) and EnsAD (Paris), and in the 'Action' programme (2018–2021), in partnership with the Ecole de la Manufacture (Lausanne) and HEM (Geneva). He is the main applicant for the 'Inhabiting the Extra-terrestrial Space' research programme (2019–2021), conducted in partnership with CNES (Paris), and supported by the SNSF.

Anne-Lyse Renon is lecturer in the Contemporary Art Department at the University of Rennes 2, an associate researcher at the Centre Alexandre Koyré (EHESS-CNRS-MNHN) and a researcher at HEAD—Genève on the 'Inhabiting the Extra-terrestrial Space' project. She holds a PhD in aesthetics from EHESS and works on design anthropology, epistemology and the history of science.